An Encyclopedia of Crazy Quilt Stitches & Motifs

by Linda Causee

Bobbie Matela, Managing Editor
Carol Wilson Mansfield, Art Director
Meredith Montross, Associate Editor
Christina Wilson, Assistant Editor
Jane Cannon Meyers, Technical Editor
Carol Wilson Mansfield, Terea Mitchell and Mary Hernandez, Illustrations
Graphic Solutions, Inc-chgo, Book Design

For a full-color catalog
including books on quilting and
ribbon embroidery, write to:

American School of Needlework®,
Consumer Division
1455 Linda Vista Drive
San Marcos, CA 92069

Some of the ribbon embroidery motifs included in this book can
also be found in the following books by the Kooler Design Studio,
published by ASN Publishing. They are reprinted by permission of
the copyright holder.

#3406 - Ribbon Embroidery Alphabets, by Barbara Baatz
#3407 - 101 Iron-On Transfers for Ribbon Embroidery,
       by Deanna Hall West
#3408 - An Encyclopedia of Ribbon Embroidery Birds,
       Butterflies, and Blossoms, by Deanna Hall West

The crystal and glass beads used on the cover crazy quilt are Mill
Hill Glass and Crystal Treasures. For more information, write to:
Gay Bowles Sales, Inc., P.O. Box 1060, Janesville, WI 53547-1060

©1997 by American School of Needlework®, Inc.; ASN Publishing, 1455 Linda Vista Drive, San Marcos, CA 92069
ISBN: 0-88195-840-9   Printed in U. S. A.   All rights reserved.   4 5 6 7 8 9

746.46
Cau
17.95
10/30/98

Introduction

So you've always thought it would be fun to make a crazy quilt! Perhaps you want to use the fabrics you saved from your daughter's childhood wardrobe. Maybe you've been collecting silks, satins and other luscious fabrics to use someday for a special crazy quilt. Chances are, you've been putting off making this quilt because it's too intimidating to cut into these irreplaceable fabrics and you're really not sure how you would like to embellish this once-in-a-lifetime quilt. (It may be called a crazy quilt, but you don't want to end up with a crazy-looking quilt!)

You'll love this book for the 90 Crazy Quilt Stitches that are illustrated with how-to instructions, pages 13 to 58. There are enough stitches and variations to use a new creative stitch for each seam of your patchwork. This is a wonderful reference for anyone who enjoys needlework. In addition there are eleven Ribbon Motifs (with instruction for the stitches used), pages 59 to 68, that are wonderful for adding dimension to your crazy patchwork. For each ribbon motif we've included a stitching diagram to use as a blueprint for creating beautiful ribbonwork.

It helps to refer to the photographs when stitching, but if your stitches don't look exactly like the photographed stitches, there's no need to be concerned. Every time a stitcher picks up needle and thread (or ribbon), the stitches tend to look slightly different. The results, however, are always beautiful!

This book is not intended to be the definitive book on creating crazy quilts, but rather a compendium of stitches. We have, however, presented all the background information you need to get started in making your own unique crazy quilt. Learn what's what in Supplies for Crazy Quilts on page 4, then go on to Foundation Patchwork on pages 5 to 7.

Crazy patchwork is the technique in quiltmaking where irregularly-shaped pieces of fabric are sewn together to create a wonderful collage of colors and textures. It is generally agreed that crazy patchwork began in America in the late nineteenth century during the Victorian Era.

Crazy quilts were made mainly for decorative purposes rather than practical purposes since most of the fabric used was not washable. Crazy quilts were also made as special mementos of important events. Dates of birthdays, weddings and deaths were often embroidered on the quilts with small scraps of clothing from a wedding dress or christening gown incorporated into the patchwork.

Crazy patchwork was done on a fabric base or foundation that was usually muslin. A center piece was placed on the foundation and other pieces were placed around it, sewing the piece directly to the foundation in a Log Cabin style. Fancy fabrics such as silks, brocades, satins, and velvets, most often from scraps of clothing and fine linen, were used. Decorative embroidery stitches then surrounded appliquéd and painted motifs within the patchwork. Women also used pieces of lace, ribbons, flags, beads and buttons to embellish their crazy patchwork. Spiders and webs were often incorporated into the crazy quilt as they were considered a symbol of good luck when used in needlework.

Crazy quilts were not quilts in the true sense, since they were not really quilted. Many of the fabrics used for the patchwork were too thick to sew a Running Stitch through, so the quilts were either tied or tacked.

By the beginning of the twentieth century, the interest in crazy quilts tapered off as quickly as it began and renewed interest in more practical quilts took over.

Crazy quilting is gaining in popularity today as an art form in many of the same ways as in the Victorian era. Silks, satins, brocades, as well as cottons are being used with lace, buttons, charms and beads to create true works of art. Silk ribbon embroidery adds a new and exciting dimension to the classic elegance of thread embroidery.

Supplies for Crazy Quilts

Fabrics

Crazy quilts can be made using fancy fabrics such as silks, satins, velvets or brocades, as well as wools, cottons, or just about anything that fits into the color scheme and design of your crazy quilt. Prints as well as solids can also be used. The important thing to remember is to use a variety of fabrics to achieve a balanced look. You will also want to use fabrics that will show off, not take away from, the fancy embroidery stitches that will be added to your crazy quilt.

Embroidery Threads

A wide variety of threads can be used for crazy quilt stitches. Six-strand cotton floss, rayon floss, pearl cotton, silk buttonhole twist, ribbon floss, or metallics are all suitable. Use colors that will show off your embroidery to its best advantage—light colors on dark fabrics and dark colors on light fabrics. Instructions for the embroidery stitches are on pages 13 to 58.

Ribbon Embroidery

Ribbon embroidery will add a soft, three dimensional touch to your crazy quilt. Silk and the recently manufactured silk substitutes (silky polyester) can be used. For embroidery, 4mm is the most common width used, but ribbon also comes in 2mm and 7mm widths.

Work with ribbon cut into 10"-12" pieces. Embroidery ribbon is relatively fragile, and during the stitching process, the ribbon can be easily damaged if longer pieces are used.

The stitches for ribbon embroidery are similar to those used for thread embroidery. Instructions for the ribbon stitches used in this book are found on pages 59 to 63.

Needles

Due to the variety of fabrics and threads being used for crazy quilts, it is best to have several different types and sizes of needles. Crewel, tapestry and chenille needles all can be used for thread as well as ribbon embroidery. Crewel needles, sizes 6-8, or chenille needles, sizes 18-24, are best for heavier fabrics, such as velvet, and can also be used for ribbon embroidery. Tapestry needles, sizes 24-26, are also suitable for ribbon embroidery.

Embellishments

A wide assortment of embellishments can be added to your crazy quilt for those special touches. Glass seed beads, pebble beads, crystal beads, buttons, laces, charms—the possibilities are endless. Seed beads can be used, as we did on the front cover quilt, in place of French or Colonial Knots.

Frames and Hoops

The best embroidery and ribbon embroidery results are achieved when using a frame or hoop to hold the fabric taut while stitching. Use the size hoop you are most comfortable working with. But remember, if embellishing your crazy quilt with beads, buttons or charms, use a hoop or frame that is large enough so that it doesn't have to be moved during stitching, or add those embellishments last.

Foundation Patchwork

Crazy patchwork is done on a foundation that can be a lightweight cotton, muslin or interfacing. The pattern can be planned or random. Although your patchwork design can be sewn to a blank foundation, it is easier if you have a definite plan and draw the stitching lines onto the foundation. The fabric pieces are placed on the unmarked side of the foundation, while the sewing is done along the marked lines on the opposite side.

1. Start with a shape, such as a pentagon, in the center of the foundation, **Fig 1**.

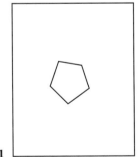

Fig 1

2. Draw stitching lines spiraling around the center shape in an irregular manner, numbering each space in the order of stitching, **Fig 2**.

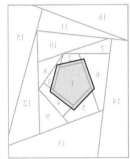

Fig 2

3. Cut a piece of fabric that is large enough to cover and overlap the center shape; place fabric on the unmarked side of the foundation making sure that fabric piece overlaps the center shape on all sides, **Fig 3**. Pin in place. **Note:** *Hold foundation up to a light source if you cannot see through your foundation.*

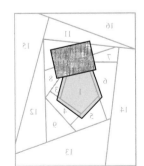

Fig 3

4. Place a second piece of fabric right sides together with first piece. **Note:** *Double check to see if fabric piece chosen will cover space 2 completely by folding it along line between space 1 and 2,* **Fig 4**.

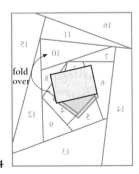

fold over

Fig 4

5

5. Turn foundation with marked side facing you and fold foundation forward along line between spaces 1 and 2; trim both pieces about ¼" above fold line, **Fig 5**.

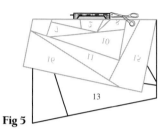

Fig 5

6. With marked side of foundation still facing you, sew along line between spaces 1 and 2, **Fig 6**; begin and end stitching two to three stitches beyond line.

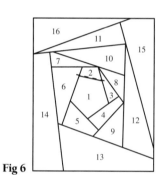

Fig 6

7. Turn foundation over. Open piece 2 and finger press seam, **Fig 7**. Pin in place.

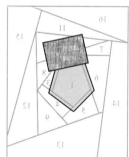

Fig 7

8. Turn foundation with marked side facing you; fold foundation forward along line between spaces 2 and 3 and trim piece 2 about ¼" from fold, **Fig 8**.

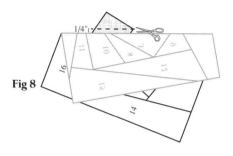

Fig 8

9. Place fabric 3 right side down even with just-trimmed edge, **Fig 9**.

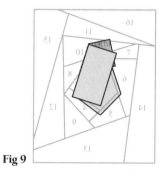

Fig 9

10. Turn foundation to marked side and sew along line between spaces 1 and 2 and 3; begin and end sewing two or three stitches beyond line, **Fig 10**.

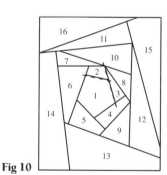

Fig 10

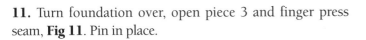

11. Turn foundation over, open piece 3 and finger press seam, **Fig 11**. Pin in place.

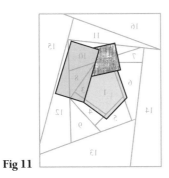

Fig 11

12. Turn foundation with marked side facing you; fold foundation forward along line between spaces 1, 3, and 4. If previous stitching makes it difficult to fold foundation forward, fold it as far as it will go and trim to about 1/4" from drawn line, **Fig 12**.

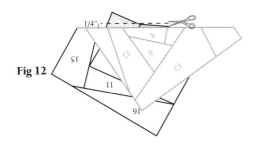

Fig 12

13. Continue trimming and sewing pieces in numerical order until entire foundation is covered. Press stitched foundation, then trim fabric even with outside line of foundation, **Fig 13**, to finish, **Fig 14**.

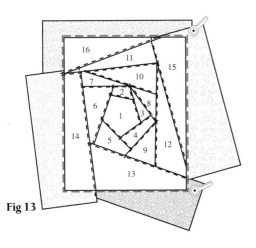

Fig 13

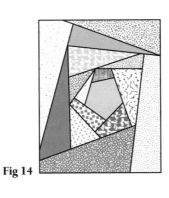

Fig 14

How to Use This Book

The stitches and ribbon motifs shown on the front cover are labeled below. This cover piece displays only 35 of the 90 stitches and seven of the eleven ribbon motifs included in this book.

The numbers refer to the stitch or motif used. You will find each of the 90 stitches worked individually in color on pages 9 to 12. And on the back cover, you will find all eleven ribbon motifs. Detailed directions on how to work each stitch are found on pages 13 to 58; directions for each motif, including the ribbon stitches, are on pages 59 to 68.

To make it easy to reproduce these stitches on your own crazy quilt, we have included step-by-step illustrations for each one. When working the stitches from the illustrations, note that the thread that is in progress is shown lighter than the finished portion of the stitch.

When working your stitches on your own crazy quilt, consider using beads or charms for added dimension. On our cover, we used glass seed beads in several stitches to replace French or Colonial Knots. We also used glass and crystal beads to enhance and add interest to the design.

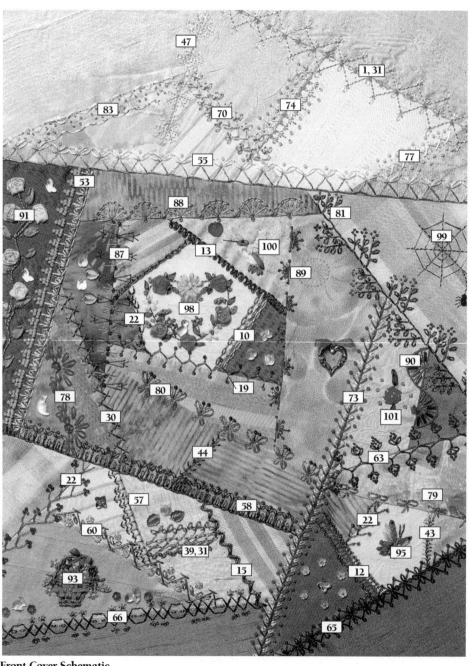

Front Cover Schematic

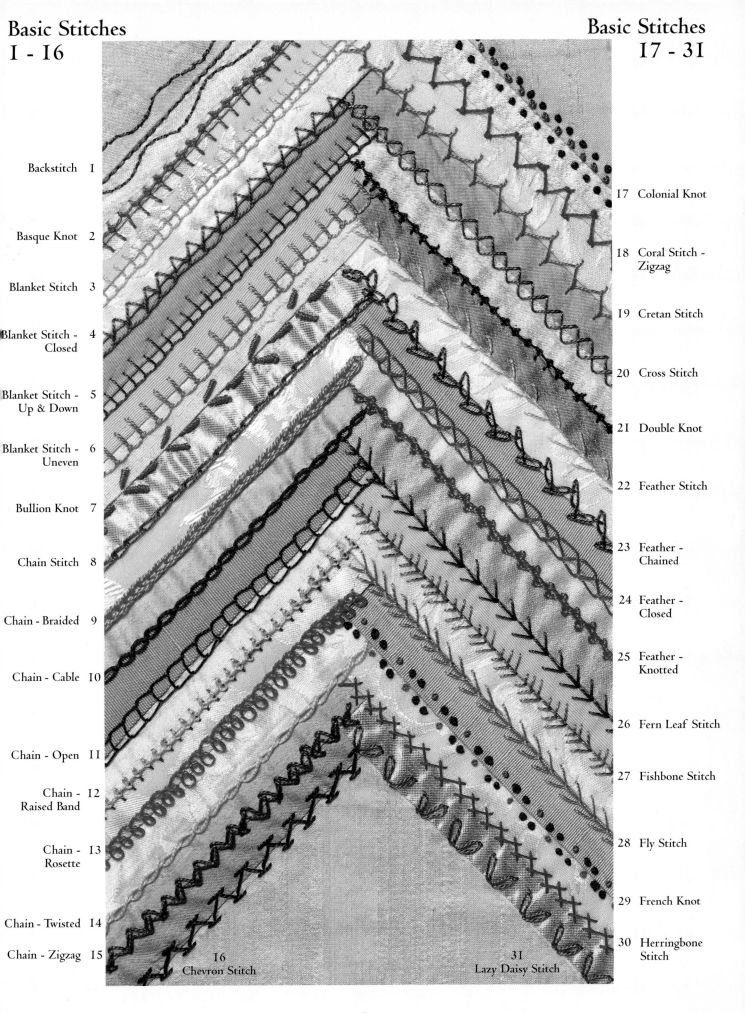

Backstitch 1

Basque Knot 2

Blanket Stitch 3

Blanket Stitch - 4
Closed

Blanket Stitch - 5
Up & Down

Blanket Stitch - 6
Uneven

Bullion Knot 7

Chain Stitch 8

Chain - Braided 9

Chain - Cable 10

Chain - Open 11

Chain - 12
Raised Band

Chain - 13
Rosette

Chain - Twisted 14

Chain - Zigzag 15

16
Chevron Stitch

17 Colonial Knot

18 Coral Stitch -
Zigzag

19 Cretan Stitch

20 Cross Stitch

21 Double Knot

22 Feather Stitch

23 Feather -
Chained

24 Feather -
Closed

25 Feather -
Knotted

26 Fern Leaf Stitch

27 Fishbone Stitch

28 Fly Stitch

29 French Knot

30 Herringbone
Stitch

31
Lazy Daisy Stitch

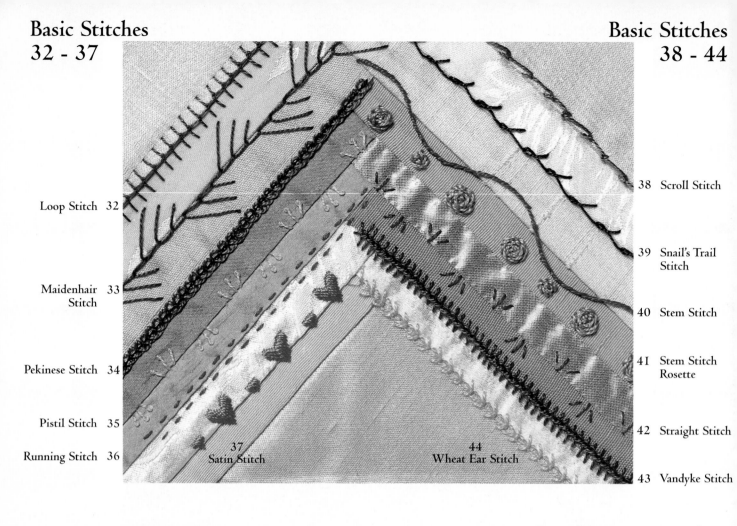

Loop Stitch 32

Maidenhair Stitch 33

Pekinese Stitch 34

Pistil Stitch 35

Running Stitch 36

37 Satin Stitch

44 Wheat Ear Stitch

38 Scroll Stitch

39 Snail's Trail Stitch

40 Stem Stitch

41 Stem Stitch Rosette

42 Straight Stitch

43 Vandyke Stitch

Combination Stitches
45 - 48

Combination Stitches
49 - 53

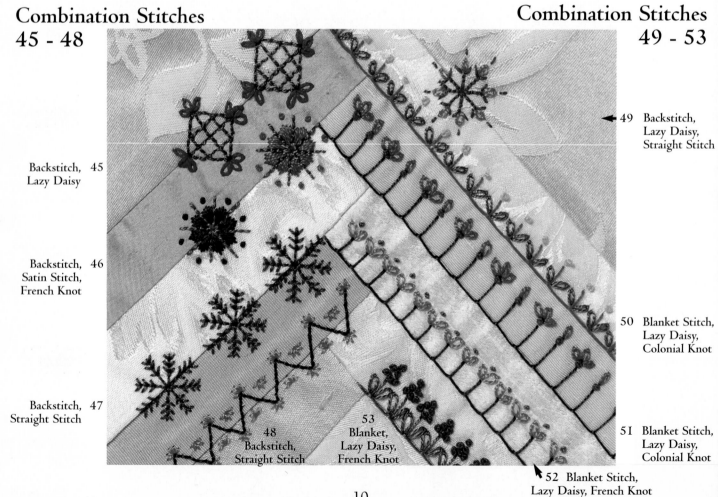

Backstitch, Lazy Daisy 45

Backstitch, Satin Stitch, French Knot 46

Backstitch, Straight Stitch 47

48 Backstitch, Straight Stitch

53 Blanket, Lazy Daisy, French Knot

49 Backstitch, Lazy Daisy, Straight Stitch

50 Blanket Stitch, Lazy Daisy, Colonial Knot

51 Blanket Stitch, Lazy Daisy, Colonial Knot

52 Blanket Stitch, Lazy Daisy, French Knot

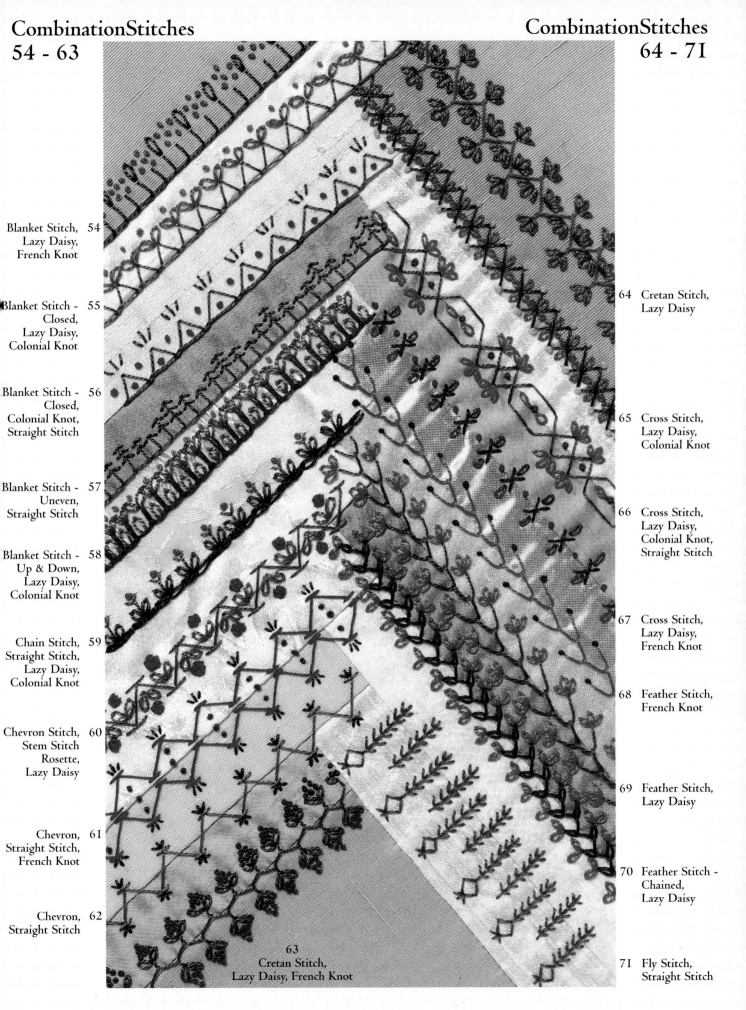

Blanket Stitch, 54
Lazy Daisy,
French Knot

Blanket Stitch - 55
Closed,
Lazy Daisy,
Colonial Knot

Blanket Stitch - 56
Closed,
Colonial Knot,
Straight Stitch

Blanket Stitch - 57
Uneven,
Straight Stitch

Blanket Stitch - 58
Up & Down,
Lazy Daisy,
Colonial Knot

Chain Stitch, 59
Straight Stitch,
Lazy Daisy,
Colonial Knot

Chevron Stitch, 60
Stem Stitch
Rosette,
Lazy Daisy

Chevron, 61
Straight Stitch,
French Knot

Chevron, 62
Straight Stitch

63
Cretan Stitch,
Lazy Daisy, French Knot

64 Cretan Stitch,
Lazy Daisy

65 Cross Stitch,
Lazy Daisy,
Colonial Knot

66 Cross Stitch,
Lazy Daisy,
Colonial Knot,
Straight Stitch

67 Cross Stitch,
Lazy Daisy,
French Knot

68 Feather Stitch,
French Knot

69 Feather Stitch,
Lazy Daisy

70 Feather Stitch -
Chained,
Lazy Daisy

71 Fly Stitch,
Straight Stitch

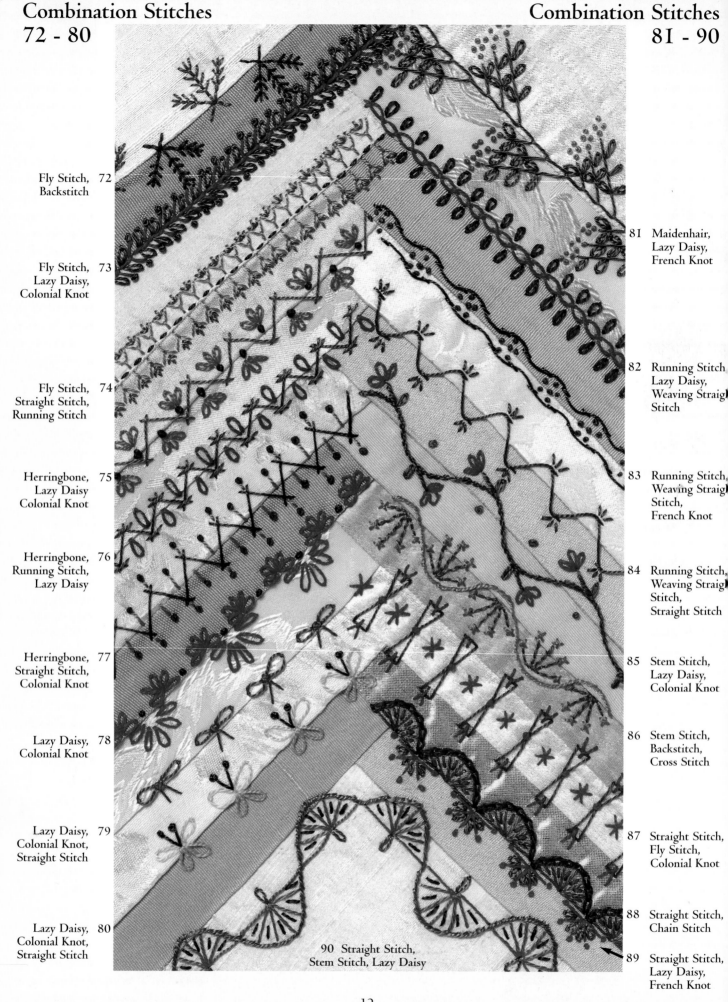

Fly Stitch, 72
Backstitch

Fly Stitch, 73
Lazy Daisy,
Colonial Knot

Fly Stitch, 74
Straight Stitch,
Running Stitch

Herringbone, 75
Lazy Daisy
Colonial Knot

Herringbone, 76
Running Stitch,
Lazy Daisy

Herringbone, 77
Straight Stitch,
Colonial Knot

Lazy Daisy, 78
Colonial Knot

Lazy Daisy, 79
Colonial Knot,
Straight Stitch

Lazy Daisy, 80
Colonial Knot,
Straight Stitch

81 Maidenhair,
Lazy Daisy,
French Knot

82 Running Stitch
Lazy Daisy,
Weaving Straight
Stitch

83 Running Stitch,
Weaving Straight
Stitch,
French Knot

84 Running Stitch,
Weaving Straight
Stitch,
Straight Stitch

85 Stem Stitch,
Lazy Daisy,
Colonial Knot

86 Stem Stitch,
Backstitch,
Cross Stitch

87 Straight Stitch,
Fly Stitch,
Colonial Knot

88 Straight Stitch,
Chain Stitch

89 Straight Stitch,
Lazy Daisy,
French Knot

90 Straight Stitch,
Stem Stitch, Lazy Daisy

Basic Stitches

¹Backstitch

Bring needle up at 1, a stitch length away from beginning of design line. Stitch back down at 2, at beginning of line. Bring needle up at 3, then stitch back down to meet previous stitch at 1. Continue in this manner, stitching backward on surface to meet previous stitch. Backstitch can be worked along curved or straight lines.

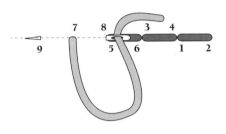

²Basque Knot

The Basque Knot is worked along two imaginary parallel lines. Come up at 1, go down at 2 along top imaginary line and come back up at 3 (below and even with 2) along bottom imaginary line. Bring needle over top of and under first stitch; pull through gently. Make a clockwise loop and again bring needle over top and under first stitch (to the left of first stitch), over loop. Pull to form a knot. Continue next stitch to the left of first stitch going down at 4 and emerging at 5.

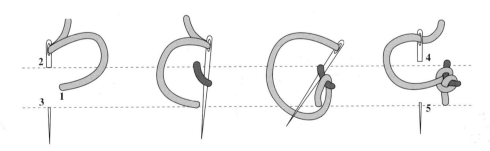

3 Blanket Stitch

Bring the needle up at 1 and reinsert needle at 2 (diagonally to the right of 1). Bring needle up at 3 (down and slightly to left of 2) keeping the thread under the point of the needle. Pull thread through to form stitch. Continue working from left to right keeping stitches the same distance apart and the same height.

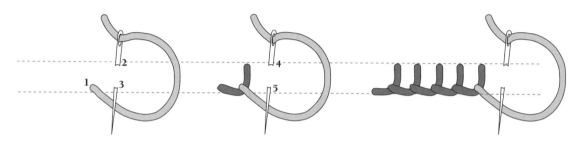

4 Blanket Stitch-Closed

The Closed Blanket Stitch is similar to the regular Blanket Stitch except that the tops of the stitches are worked into the same hole (2) to form a triangular shape. Bring the needle up at 1. Loop thread to the right and insert needle at 2. Bring needle back up at 3, making sure needle goes over loop and pull into place. Go down at 4 (same hole as 2) and come up at 5 to form the triangle. Continue in same manner, working left to right.

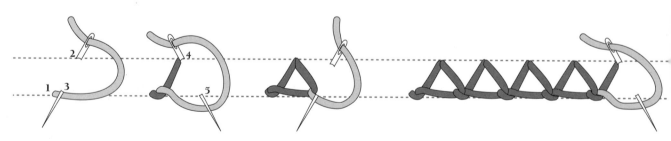

^{5}Blanket Stitch–Uneven

Begin this stitch the same as the regular Blanket Stitch. Come up at 1, down at 2 and, holding thread with thumb of non-stitching hand, emerge at 3 (slightly to left of 2 and slightly above 1). For the second stitch, go down at 4 (above first stitch) and emerge at 5. Continue in same manner adjusting height of each stitch as desired.

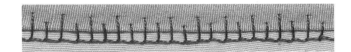

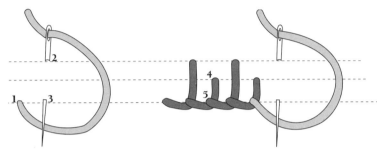

^{6}Blanket Stitch–Up & Down

Bring needle up at 1; hold thread down with thumb of non-stitching hand. Go down at 2 and bring up at 3 keeping tip of needle over the thread. Go down at 4 (next to, but not in 3) and emerge at 5 (next to, but not in 2). Pull thread down until stitch is formed. Continue in same manner working left to right.

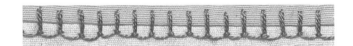

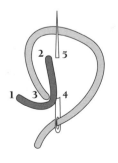

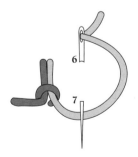

15

⁷Bullion Knot

Come up at 1, pulling needle completely through. Go down at 2 and re-emerge at 1; do not pull needle all the way through. Wrap thread around top of needle 5 or 6 times (or until length of twists equals the space between 1 and 2). Pull needle through, holding twists with other hand, close to fabric. Go down at 2, pulling firmly to shape knot.

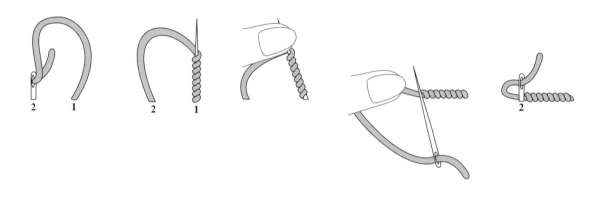

⁸Chain Stitch

Bring needle up at 1, form a counterclockwise loop and go down at 2 (same hole as 1), holding loop with left thumb. Come up at 3 bringing the tip of the needle over the loop. Repeat stitch to form a chain. The chain can be worked horizontally, vertically, or along a curve. End chain by making a small stitch over final loop.

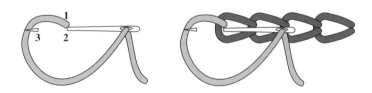

9 Chain Stitch-Braided

Make a small stitch coming up at 1 and going down at 2; emerge at 3. Pass needle under small stitch from right to left and go down at 4 (same hole as 3); emerge at 5. Pass needle under original small stitch and go down at 6 (same hole as 5). Emerge at 7, pass needle under first chain, and go down at 8 (same hole as 7). Continue in same manner working from top to bottom passing needle under the chain made before the previous chain.

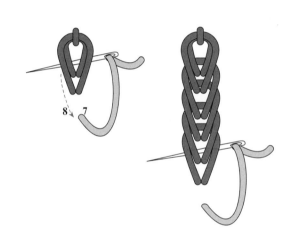

10 Chain Stitch-Cable

Bring needle up at 1; wrap thread once around needle. Go down at 2, pull snugly and emerge at 3 with tip of needle over thread. Pull thread gently to complete stitch. Continue in same manner working top to bottom.

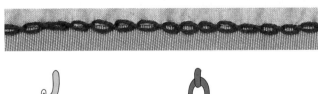

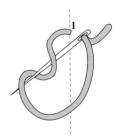

11 Chain Stitch-Open

Come up at 1 and down at 2 (even with 1) forming a
loop. Emerge at 3 (directly below 1) with needle tip
over loop; leave loop loose. Go down at 4 above loop
(directly below 2 and to the right of 3) and emerge at
5. Pull thread to form stitch, leaving loop loose.
Continue in same manner working from top to bottom along two imaginary parallel lines.

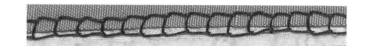

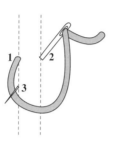
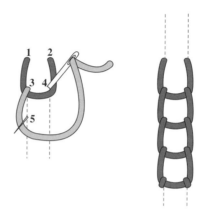

12 Chain Stitch-Raised Band

Work the desired number of equal-length straight
stitches that are spaced rather closely together. With
another thread (a different color, if desired), come up
at 1, pass needle under first straight stitch, toward the
left of 1. Form a loop and coming from the top, pass
needle under first Straight Stitch toward the right of 1,
with needle tip above loop. Pull through to form knot.
Continue stitching in same manner, ending by stitching down over last loop.

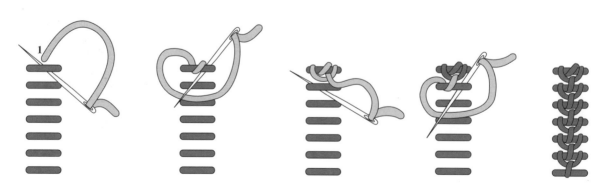

13 Chain Stitch-Rosette

This stitch is worked right to left. Bring needle up at 1, form a counterclockwise loop, and go down at 2; emerge at 3 with tip of needle over loop. Pull needle through loop completely, but not too tightly. For next stitch, pass needle under top right thread (to the left of 1); form loop and continue next stitch in same manner.

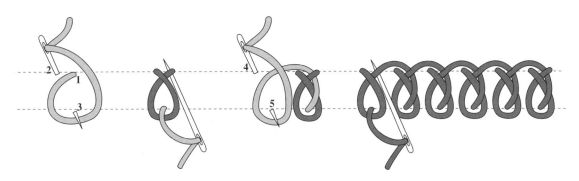

14 Chain Stitch-Twisted

Come up at 1 along an imaginary line, form a counterclockwise loop, go down at 2 (slightly below and to the left of 1); emerge at 3 (directly below 1 along imaginary line) with tip of needle on top of loop. Pull thread through and continue next stitch in same manner.

15 Chain Stitch-Zigzag

Come up at 1 and form a counterclockwise loop; go down at 2 (same hole as 1) and come back up at 3 (to left of and below 1) with tip of needle over loop. Pull needle through completely and form another loop; go down at 4 (same hole as 3), piercing lower end of first loop. Come back up at 5 (to the left of and even with 1). Continue in same manner for length desired.

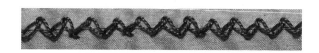

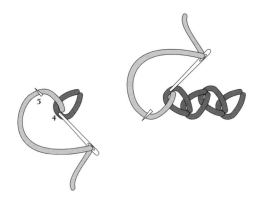

16 Chevron Stitch

This stitch is worked from left to right between two imaginary parallel design lines. It can be used as a border or filling. Bring needle up at 1 and down at 2; hold the thread down with thumb of non-stitching hand and make a small stitch bringing needle up at 3 (halfway between 1 and 2). Reinsert needle at 4, diagonally above 3, and bring out at 5. Insert needle at 6 keeping thread above needle and bring out at 7 (same hole as 4). Insert at 8 and come up at 9. Continue working stitch in same manner.

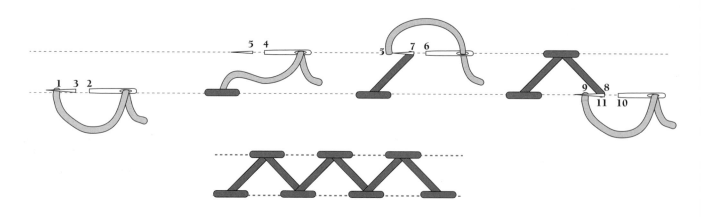

17 Colonial Knot

Come up at 1, make a clockwise loop and slip point of needle beneath thread from left to right. Bring thread around point of needle in a figure eight motion. Insert needle at 2 (next to, but not into 1); pull thread while pulling needle through to back of fabric.

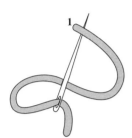

18 Coral Stitch-Zigzag

Come up at 1 and go down at 2 (close to 1). Form a small counterclockwise loop and emerge at 3 with tip of needle on top of loop; pull needle completely through. Form a small clockwise loop below and to the left of first knot; go down at 4 (to right of loop) and emerge through loop at 5 with tip of needle over loop. Continue in a zigzag manner along imaginary parallel lines for desired length.

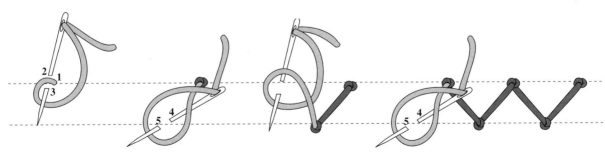

19 Cretan Stitch

Come up at 1. Go down at 2 (above and to the right of 1) and emerge at 3 (directly below and desired distance from 2) with tip of needle over top of thread. Insert needle at 4 and emerge at 5 (directly above 4 and the same distance as between 2 and 3) with tip of needle over top of thread. Continue working in same manner along pairs of imaginary parallel lines, keeping vertical stitches evenly spaced.

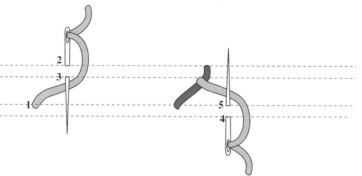

20 Cross Stitch

Bring needle up at 1 and down at 2. Complete the stitch by coming up at 3 and down at 4. When doing a row of Cross Stitches, make all stitches from 1 to 2 first, going from left to right. Complete row by working from right to left along two imaginary parallel lines with stitches from bottom right to upper left.

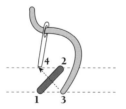

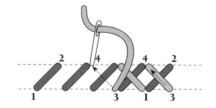

21 Double Knot

Come up at 1, go down at 2 (to the right of and below 1) and emerge at 3 (directly across from 2); pull needle through. Pass needle over top and under stitch just made; pull needle through. Form counterclockwise loop and pass needle under beginning stitch and over loop. Pull thread to form knot. Continue with next stitch in same manner.

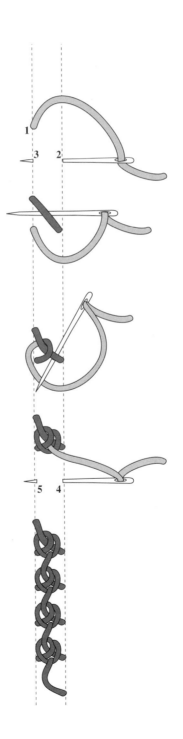

22 Feather Stitch

Come up at 1 and go down at 2 (to left of and even with 1); emerge at 3 (below and between 1 and 2) with tip of needle over thread. Pull thread completely through and go down at 4; emerge at 5 (below 3 and 4 and directly under 1). Pull thread completely through and continue stitching in same manner. End by making a small stitch over last loop.

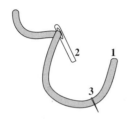

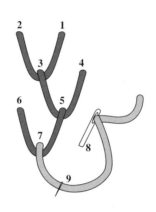

23 Feather Stitch-Chained

Begin stitch as for Chain Stitch (page 16). Come up at 1, loop thread and go down again at 2 (same hole as 1); emerge at 3 (below and to the left of 1), with tip of needle over thread. Pull thread through and go down at 4 making a slanted Straight Stitch. Come up at 5, form loop and go down at 6 (same hole as 5), emerging at 7 to form next chain. Go down at 8 making a slanted Straight Stitch. Continue in same manner forming a zigzag pattern with Straight Stitches.

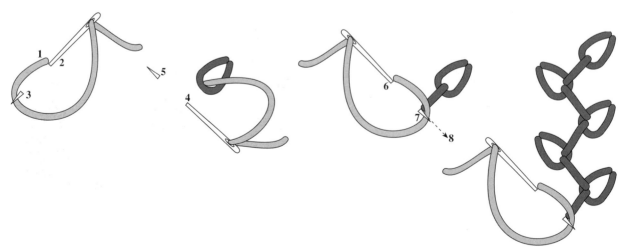

24 Feather Stitch–Closed

Come up at 1 and go down at 2 (to the right of and slightly above 1); emerge at 3 (directly below 2) with tip of needle over thread. Pull needle through completely and go down at 4 (next to and slightly below 1); emerge at 5 (directly below 4). Continue in same manner for desired length.

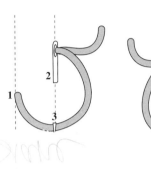

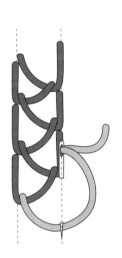

25 Feather St[

Come up at 1, form a [   ] down at 2 (above and [   ] (below and slightly to the left of 2), with tip of needle over thread. Pull needle through and form a clockwise loop; go down at 4 and emerge at 5 going through loop. Pull needle through and form a counterclockwise loop; go down at 6 and emerge at 7 going through loop. Pull needle through and continue stitching in same manner.

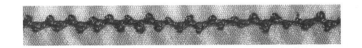

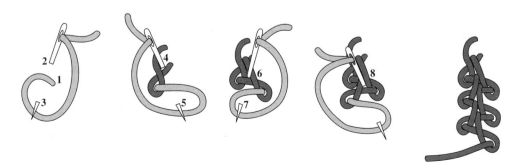

26 *Fern Leaf Stitch*

Bring needle up at 1 and down at 2. Come up again at 1, down at 3, up again at 1 and down at 4. Continue working three Straight Stitches in same manner following design line. This stitch is used for sprays and leaf veins.

27 *Fishbone Stitch*

This stitch can be used to fill in shapes. Mark desired shape on fabric. Bring needle up at 1 and down the desired distance. Come back up at 2 and down over lower end of first stitch. Come up at 3 and down covering lower edge of previous stitch. Continue in same manner alternating from side to side.

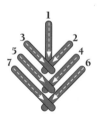

28 *Fly Stitch*

Bring the needle up at 1 and down at 2; keep stitch loose. Come up at 3 and pull thread to form a "V"; go down at 4. Continue in same manner going vertically or horizontally.

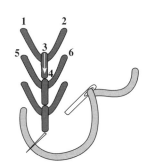

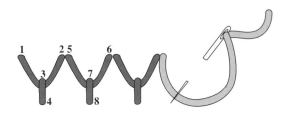

29 *French Knot*

Bring needle up at 1. Wrap thread once around shaft of needle. Insert point of needle at 2 (close to, but not into 1). Hold knot down as you pull needle through to the back of fabric.

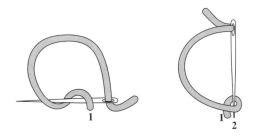

30 *Herringbone Stitch*

Bring needle up at 1 along an imaginary line. Insert needle at 2, diagonally above 1 and bring up at 3. Reinsert needle at 4 and bring out at 5. Continue in this manner working from left to right. This stitch can be used as a border or a filler.

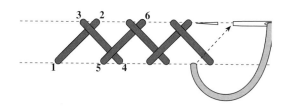

31 *Lazy Daisy Stitch*

Bring needle up at 1 and reinsert needle at 2 (same hole as 1). Pull thread until loop is desired length. Bring needle up at 3 (inside loop) and pull thread until loop is desired length. Stitch down over the loop at 4.

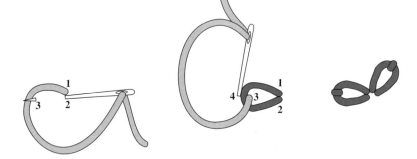

32 Loop Stitch

Come up at 1, go down at 2 (above and to the left
of 1); come back up at 3 (directly below 2). Pass
needle over and under first stitch and pull needle
through with tip over top of thread to form knot.
For next stitch go down at 4 and come up at 5. Pass
needle over and under stitch just made and pull
through with tip of needle over top of thread.
Continue in same manner for desired length.

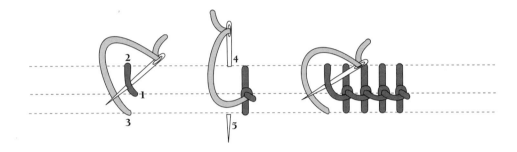

33 Maidenhair Stitch

Come up at 1 and down at 2 (to the left of and even
with 1); emerge at 3 (below and to the left of 1)
bringing tip of needle over thread. Pull needle
through and go down at 4 (to the left of and even
with 2); emerge at 5 (below and to the left of 3). Pull
needle through and go down at 6 (to the left of and
even with 4) and emerge at 7 (below and to left of 5).
Pull needle through and go down at 8 (to right and
even with 7) and emerge at 9. Continue in same
manner for two more stitches, then do alternating
groups of three stitches for desired length.

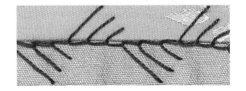

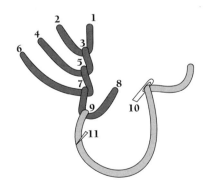

34 Pekinese Stitch

Make a row of small Backstitches (page 13). Using a thread of the same (or contrasting) color, come up at A and pass needle under second Backstitch from the left; loop thread counterclockwise and pass needle under first Backstitch with tip of needle over top of loop, leaving stitch loose. Continue looping stitches along entire Backstitch.

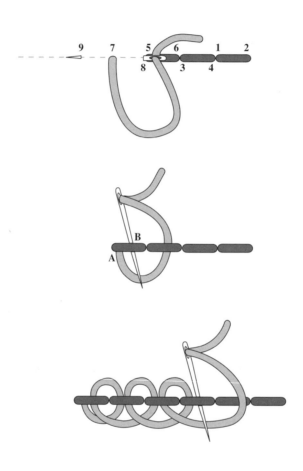

35 *Pistil Stitch*

Bring needle up at 1, wrap thread twice around shaft of needle. Swing point of needle clockwise and reinsert at 2, desired distance from 1. Pull wrapping thread around needle and hold with thumb and forefinger of non-stitching hand while pulling needle through to back of fabric.

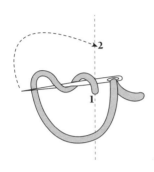

36 *Running Stitch*

Work stitches from right to left. Bring needle up at 1 and down at 2. Continue stitching, keeping length of stitches the same as the spaces between.

37 *Satin Stitch*

Come up at 1 and down at 2. Continue with Straight Stitches very close together to fill desired pattern.

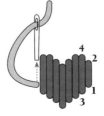

38 *Scroll Stitch*

Come up at 1. Loop thread clockwise to the right of 1; hold loop in place with thumb of non-stitching hand. Go down at 2 and up at 3 (to left of and below 2) making a small stitch inside of loop. Pull thread to tighten loop and pull needle through while holding tightened loop in place. Continue stitching left to right for desired length.

39 *Snail's Trail Stitch*

Come up at 1 and make a counterclockwise loop (to left of 1). Holding down loop with thumb of non-stitching hand, go down at 2 (above and to left of 1) and emerge at 3 (to left of and even with 1) with tip of needle over loop. Pull needle through and continue stitching in same manner.

40 *Stem Stitch*

Bring needle up at 1. Hold thread down with the thumb of your non-stitching hand. Reinsert needle at 2 and bring up at 3, about halfway between 1 and 2. Pull the thread through and continue in this manner with thread held below stitching. Work in straight or curved lines.

41 *Stem Stitch Rosette*

Start with three Stem Stitches (above) in the center; come up at 1, down at 2 and back up at 3. Continue adding stitches spiraling outward to desired size.

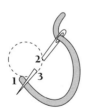

42 *Straight Stitch*

Come up at 1 and down at 2. Straight Stitches can be varying sizes and spaced regularly or irregularly.

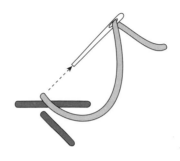

43 *Vandyke Stitch*

Come up at 1 and down at 2; come back up at 3 (to the left of and even with 2) and go down at 4. Come up at 5 (directly below and even with 1) and pass needle under area where threads cross going from right to left. Pull needle through, keeping loop loose. Go down at 6 (directly below and even with 4) and back up at 7 (directly below and even with 5). Pass needle under previous crossed stitches and go down at 8. Continue in same manner for desired length.

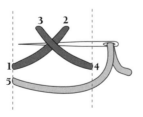

44 Wheat Ear Stitch

Come up at 1 and down at 2, up at 3 (even with and to the right of 1) and down at 4 (same hole as 2). Emerge at 5, directly below 2 and 4 (about same distance as the length between 1 and 2 and 3 and 4). Pull needle through completely and loop needle under the two stitches just made going from right to left. Go down at 6 (same hole as 5). Come back up at 7 and continue next stitch in same manner.

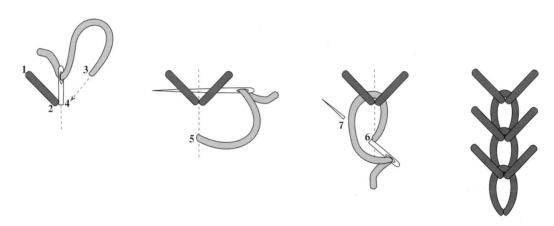

Combination Stitches

45 Backstitch with Lazy Daisy Stitch

Outline diamond shape and fill in center grid with Backstitch (page 13). Stitch three Lazy Daisy Stitches (page 28) at each corner. Repeat for each combination stitch.

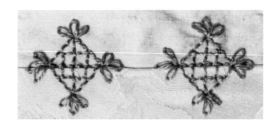

46 Backstitch with Satin Stitch and French Knot

Stitch four spokes with Backstitch (page 13). Fill in pie-shaped areas with Satin Stitch (page 31); finish with a French Knot (page 27) above each point of Satin Stitch. Repeat for each combination stitch.

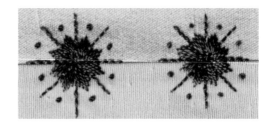

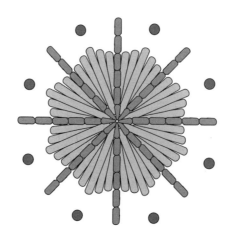

47 *Backstitch with Straight Stitch*

Stitch four spokes with Backstitch (page 13). Work Straight Stitches (page 34) on both sides of each spoke. Repeat for each combination stitch.

48 *Backstitch with Straight Stitch*

Backstitch (page 13) the zigzag lines of design; work five tiny Straight Stitches (page 34) at tip of each line and between the lines.

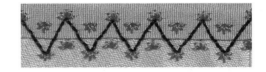

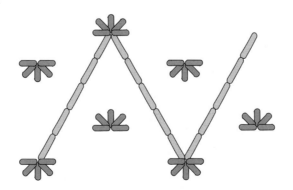

49 Backstitch with Lazy Daisy Stitch and Straight Stitch

Stitch four spokes with Backstitch (page 13); at end of each spoke, work a Lazy Daisy Stitch (page 28) with a small Straight Stitch (page 34) above and on each side of Lazy Daisy Stitch.

50 Blanket Stitch with Lazy Daisy Stitch and Colonial Knot

Work a row of Blanket Stitches (page 14). Work two Lazy Daisy Stitches (page 28) along lower edge of each Blanket Stitch. Stitch a Colonial Knot (page 21) above each Blanket Stitch.

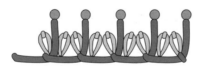

51 Blanket Stitch with Lazy Daisy Stitch and Colonial Knot

Work a row of Blanket Stitches (page 14). Work a Colonial Knot (page 21) above each Blanket Stitch. Above every other Colonial Knot, work one Lazy Daisy Stitch (page 28); above remaining Colonial Knots, work a cluster of three Lazy Daisy Stitches.

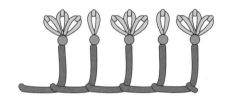

52 Blanket Stitch with Lazy Daisy Stitch and French Knot

Work a row of Blanket Stitches (page 14). At the top of each stitch, work two Lazy Daisy Stitches (page 28); complete stitch with French Knot (page 27) directly above each Blanket Stitch, between the Lazy Daisy Stitches.

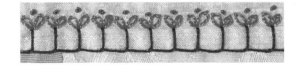

53 Blanket Stitch with Lazy Daisy Stitch and Colonial Knot

Work a row of Blanket Stitches (page 14). Work two Lazy Daisy Stitches (page 28) at base of each Blanket Stitch. Stitch three rows of Colonial Knots (page 21) above each Blanket Stitch.

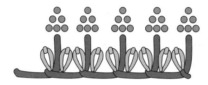

54 Blanket Stitch with Lazy Daisy Stitch and French Knot

Work a row of Blanket Stitches (page 14), then work a Lazy Daisy Stitch (page 28) above every other Blanket Stitch. Work six French Knots (page 27) above each remaining Blanket Stitch.

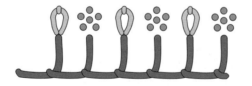

55 Blanket Stitch-Closed with Lazy Daisy Stitch and Colonial Knot

Work a row of Blanket Stitches-Closed (page 14). Work two Lazy Daisy Stitches (page 28) above each point of Blanket Stitch and a Colonial Knot (page 21) between each pair of Lazy Daisy Stitches.

56 Blanket Stitch-Closed with Colonial Knot and Straight Stitch

Work a row of Blanket Stitches-Closed (page 14). Work three Straight Stitches (page 34) above point of each Blanket Stitch triangle. Work Colonial Knots (page 21) inside and outside each triangle.

57 Blanket Stitch–Uneven with Straight Stitch

Work a row of Blanket Stitches-Uneven (page 15). Work pairs of Straight Stitches (page 34) as shown along each upright stitch.

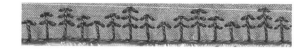

58 Blanket Stitch–Up & Down with Lazy Daisy Stitch and Colonial Knot

Work a row of Blanket Stitches-Up & Down (page 15). Work a Lazy Daisy Stitch (page 28) between each Blanket Stitch; work two Lazy Daisy Stitches above each Blanket Stitch with a Colonial Knot (page 21) between.

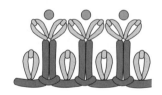

59 *Chain Stitch with Straight Stitch, Lazy Daisy Stitch and Colonial Knot*

Work a row of Chain Stitches (page 16). Work a Straight Stitch (page 34) and two Lazy Daisy Stitches (page 28) at end of each chain stitch. Work two Straight Stitches and a Colonial Knot (page 21) above each Straight Stitch.

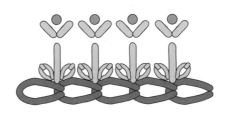

60 *Chevron Stitch with Lazy Daisy Stitch and Stem Stitch Rosette*

Begin with a row of Chevron Stitches (page 20). Work two Lazy Daisy Stitches (page 28) between each Chevron Stitch and make a Stem Stitch Rosette (page 33) above or below each pair of Lazy Daisy Stitches.

61 Chevron Stitch with Straight Stitch and French Knot

Work two rows of Chevron Stitches (page 20) stitched opposite each other. Work three Straight Stitches (page 34) above tip of each Chevron Stitch. Work three French Knots (page 27) in a row inside each stitched area.

62 Chevron Stitch and Straight Stitch

Work a row of Chevron Stitches (page 20). Work three Straight Stitches (page 34) on top of each point of Chevron Stitch.

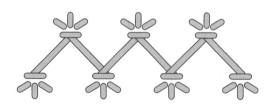

63 Cretan Stitch with Lazy Daisy Stitch and French Knot

Work a row of Cretan Stitches (page 22). Work two Lazy Daisy Stitches (page 28) above each point; work six French Knots (page 27) above each pair of Lazy Daisy Stitches.

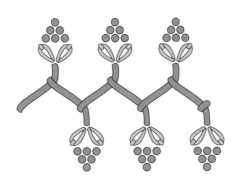

64 Cretan Stitch with Lazy Daisy Stitch

Work a row of Cretan Stitches (page 22). Work three Lazy Daisy Stitches (page 28) above and below points of each Cretan Stitch.

65 Cross Stitch with Lazy Daisy Stitch and Colonial Knot

Work desired number of large Cross Stitches (page 22). Work four Lazy Daisy Stitches (page 28) out from center of each cross. Work Colonial Knots (page 21) at corners of each cross.

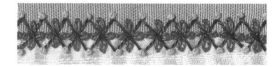

66 Cross Stitch with Lazy Daisy Stitch, Colonial Knot and Straight Stitch

Alternate three large Cross Stitches (page 22) with two long Straight Stitches (page 34). Work three Lazy Daisy Stitches (page 28) at each corner of middle Cross Stitch. Between Straight Stitches, work two Lazy Daisy Stitches and one Colonial Knot (page 21); work a Colonial Knot inside each Cross Stitch space.

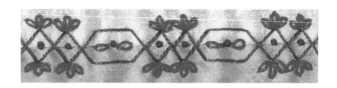

67 Cross Stitch with French Knot and Lazy Daisy Stitch

Work a row of Cross Stitches (page 22), leaving spaces between the stitches; work a French Knot (page 27) in each space. Work a Lazy Daisy Stitch (page 28) above and below each Cross Stitch.

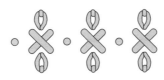

68 Feather Stitch with French Knot

Work desired length of Feather Stitches (page 24); work French Knots (page 27) at the ends of the stitches.

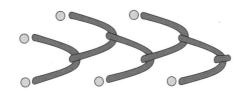

69 Feather Stitch with Lazy Daisy Stitch

Work a desired length of Feather Stitches (page 24);
work three Lazy Daisy Stitches (page 28) at the ends
of the stitches.

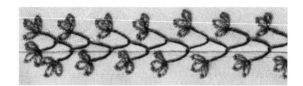

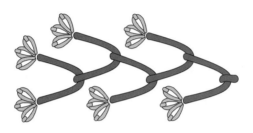

70 Feather Stitch-Chained with Lazy Daisy Stitch

Work desired length of Feather Stitches-Chained
(page 24); work two Lazy Daisy Stitches (page 28) at
end of each stitch.

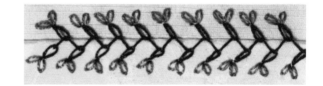

71 *Fly Stitch with Straight Stitch*

Start with a Straight Stitch (page 34), then work six Fly Stitches (page 27) in vertical rows, starting every other row one stitch lower. Work a diamond shape with Straight Stitches below the lower rows of Fly Stitches; add three Straight Stitches below each diamond.

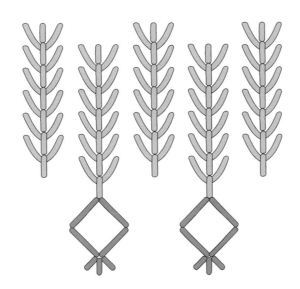

72 *Fly Stitch with Backstitch*

Start with a Backstitch (page 13), then work one row of vertical Fly Stitches (page 27); add another Backstitch at end. Stitch two rows of diagonal Fly Stitches, extending ends with Backstitches (page 13) to intersect.

73 *Fly Stitch with Lazy Daisy Stitch and Colonial Knot*

Work desired length of Fly Stitches (page 27). In between each stitch, work two Lazy Daisy Stitches (page 28). Work Colonial Knots (page 21) at ends of each Fly Stitch.

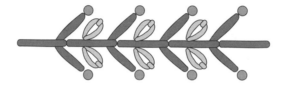

74 *Fly Stitch with Straight Stitch and Running Stitch*

Work two horizontal rows of individual Fly Stitches (page 27) opposite each other. Work Running Stitches (page 31) between rows of Fly Stitches. Work three Straight Stitches (page 34) inside Fly Stitches.

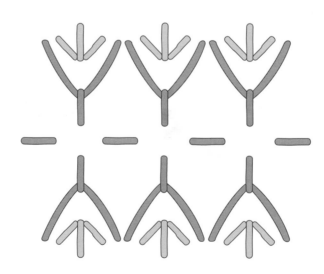

75 Herringbone Stitch with Lazy Daisy Stitch and Colonial Knot

Work Herringbone Stitch (page 28) the desired length. Work three Lazy Daisy Stitches (page 28) between the large "Vs" of Herringbone Stitches. At base of each Lazy Daisy Stitch group, stitch a Colonial Knot (page 21).

76 Herringbone Stitch with Running Stitch and Lazy Daisy Stitch

Work Herringbone Stitch (page 28) the desired length. Work Running Stitches (page 31) where Herringbone Stitches cross. Work Lazy Daisy Stitch (page 28) in each space between stitches.

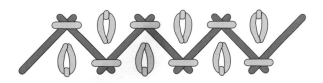

77 Herringbone Stitch with Straight Stitch and Colonial Knot

Work Herringbone Stitch (page 28) the desired length; then work Straight Stitches (page 34) above and below each stitch. Add a Colonial Knot (page 21) at end of each Straight Stitch.

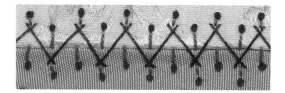

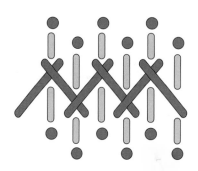

78 Lazy Daisy Stitch and Colonial Knot

Work clusters of five small Lazy Daisy Stitches (page 28) in a fan shape; work a Colonial Knot (page 21) between clusters. On opposite side, work five larger Lazy Daisy Stitches in a fan shape below every other Colonial Knot.

79 Lazy Daisy Stitch with Colonial Knot and Straight Stitch

Work two Lazy Daisy Stitches (page 28) with a Colonial Knot (page 21) in between. Add two Straight Stitches (page 34) to form tails of bow. Repeat for desired number of bows.

80 Lazy Daisy Stitch with Colonial Knot and Straight Stitch

Work four Lazy Daisy Stitches (page 28). Add two Straight Stitches (page 34) with a Colonial Knot (page 21) at end of each Straight Stitch. **Note:** *Make upper two Lazy Daisy Stitches larger than other two to form butterfly.*

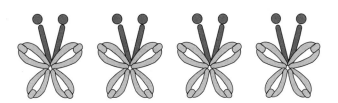

81 Maidenhair Stitch with Lazy Daisy Stitch and French Knot

Work Maidenhair Stitch (page 29) the desired length. Work Lazy Daisy Stitches (page 28) along each stitch of Maidenhair Stitches. Add cluster of four French Knots (page 27) at each end.

82 Running Stitch with Lazy Daisy Stitch and Weaving

Work a row of Running Stitches (page 31); weave two rows of thread through the Running Stitches forming a woven pattern. Work Lazy Daisy Stitches (page 28) above and below each Running Stitch.

83 Running Stitch with Weaving and French Knot

Work two rows of Running Stitches (page 31) approximately ¼" apart. Weave thread through each row of Running Stitches. In each center area, work six French Knots (page 27).

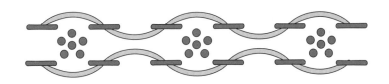

84 Running Stitch with Weaving and Straight Stitch

Work two rows of Running Stitches (page 31); weave thread through Running Stitches. Work three Straight Stitches (page 34) at top of each curve.

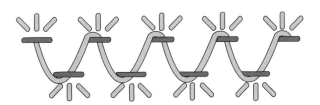

85 Stem Stitch with Lazy Daisy Stitch and Colonial Knot

Work a curving Stem Stitch (page 33) with small stems at each outside curve as shown. Work one Lazy Daisy Stitch (page 28) on each curve at base of each stem, with three Lazy Daisy Stitches at end of each stem. Add Colonial Knots (page 21) in inner curves.

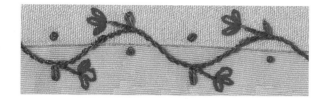

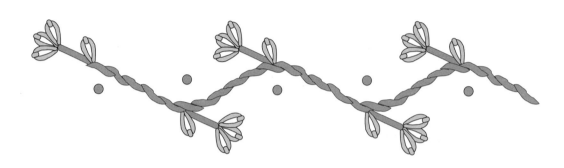

86 Stem Stitch with Backstitch and Cross Stitch

Work curving Stem Stitch (page 33) the desired length. Inside each curve, work five Backstitch (page 13) stems with a Cross Stitch (page 22) at end of each stem.

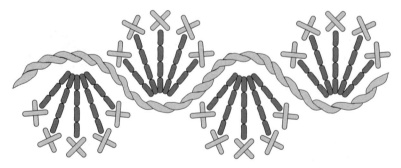

87 Straight Stitch with Fly Stitch and Colonial Knot

Work row of evenly-spaced Straight Stitch (page 34) triangles; work another row directly opposite first row with tips touching. Work a Colonial Knot (page 21) over tips of triangles. Work a Fly Stitch (page 27) centered at wide end of each triangle. Finish with three Straight Stitches between each pair of triangles.

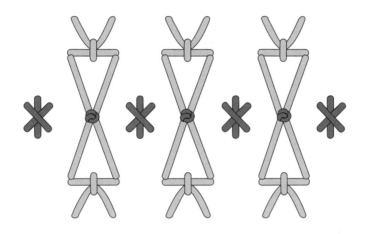

88 Straight Stitch and Chain Stitch

Work seven long Straight Stitches (page 34) meeting at one point to form a fan. Work short Straight Stitches between long Straight Stitches. Form an arc of Chain Stitches (page 16) on outer edge of long Straight Stitches.

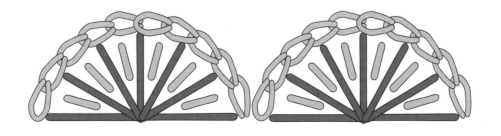

89 *Straight Stitch with Lazy Daisy Stitch and French Knot*

For each combination, work five Straight Stitches (page 34); work a French Knot (page 27) at end of each stitch. Work Lazy Daisy Stitches (page 28) between Straight Stitches.

90 *Straight Stitch with Stem Stitch and Lazy Daisy Stitch*

Work seven long Straight Stitches (page 34) forming a fan shape; add short Straight Stitches between long Straight Stitches. Work another set of Straight Stitches next to first with fan shape on opposite side. Work Stem Stitch (page 33) on outside edge of fan; add a Lazy Daisy Stitch (page 28) in center at base of fan.

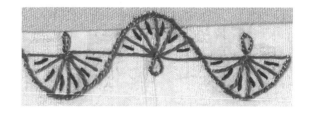

Ribbon Embroidery Stitches

Backstitch

Bring needle up at 1, a stitch length away from beginning of design line. Stitch back down at 2, at beginning of line. Bring needle up at 3, then stitch back
down to meet previous stitch. Continue, carrying ribbon forward beneath fabric and stitching backward
on the surface to meet previous stitch. Backstitch can
be worked along curving or straight lines.

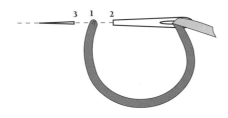

Colonial Knot

This makes a larger knot than the French Knot (page
61). Bring ribbon up at 1. Swing ribbon in a clockwise loop; follow arrow and slip point of needle
beneath ribbon from left to right. Bring ribbon
around point of needle in a figure eight motion.

Insert needle at 2, near 1; needle will be vertical.
Pull ribbon loosely around needle as you pull needle
through to back of fabric. Do not pull too tightly.

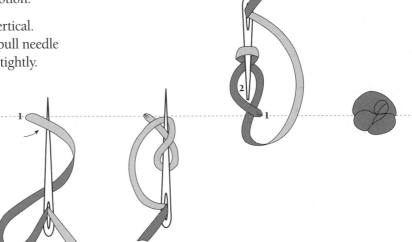

French Knot

When embroidering with ribbon, French Knots are worked more loosely than with floss or yarn. Bring needle up at 1 and wrap ribbon once or twice around shaft of needle. Swing point of needle clockwise and insert into fabric at 2, close to 1. Keep the working ribbon wrapped loosely around needle as your pull needle through to back of fabric. Release wrapping ribbon as knot is formed, and do not pull the knot too tightly. You can change the size of the French Knot by using different ribbon widths, wrapping the ribbon one or more times around the needle, and/or varying your tension.

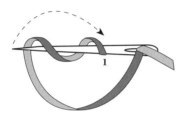

Loop Stitch

Bring needle up at 1, stitch down at 2 (close to 1), and pull ribbon part way through fabric. Insert a piece of drinking straw (or pencil, large tapestry needle, pin, etc.) through loop; pull ribbon snug to hold shape. Keep straw in place until the next petal is made in the same manner, then remove straw. If desired, these upright petals can be tacked in place.

 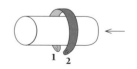

Padded Straight Stitch

Make a Straight Stitch (1-2), then work a longer Straight Stitch (3-4) directly over the first one, to create volume.

Ribbon Stitch

Bring needle up at 1 and flatten ribbon as it emerges through fabric. Extend ribbon just beyond length of stitch and insert needle through top surface of ribbon at 2. Pull ribbon gently through fabric as the sides of ribbon curl inward to form a point. Leave the curls showing by not pulling too tightly. Vary this stitch by using different ribbon widths and tension.

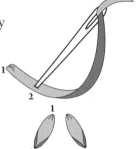

Side Ribbon Stitch

Begin as if for a Ribbon Stitch (above), but insert needle close to one edge of ribbon. Continue to gently pull until desired shape for tip is achieved.

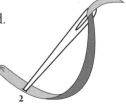

Spider Web Rose

Begin by making a Fly Stitch (page 27) with a narrow ribbon or floss, then add two extra legs (5-6 and 7-8) to create a base. End off ribbon. Bring a different ribbon up at center of web and begin weaving over and under the five legs in a circular manner until desired fullness is achieved. To end, insert needle beneath rose and pull gently through fabric; do not worry about twists—they add interest and dimension.

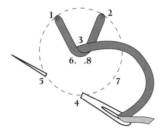

Straight Stitch

Bring needle from back of fabric at beginning point of stitch (1). Flatten ribbon with non-stitching thumb beyond intended length of the stitch, and stitch down at opposite end of stitch (2). Pull gently from 1 to 2, while keeping the stitch flat.

Weaving

This technique can be used to fill any space. Follow numerical sequence to work horizontal Straight Stitches (page 63) for the foundation.

Bring a new ribbon up at A and weave under and over the previously worked stitches, making sure ribbon does not twist; stitch down at B. Weave additional rows in alternating patterns. Continue to fill space in this manner.

The foundation can also be laid with diagonal stitches; weave on the opposite diagonal.

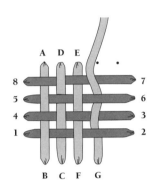 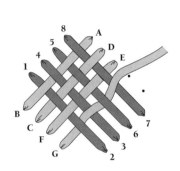

Wrapped Backstitch

Begin by working a row of Backstitches (page 60): Bring ribbon up at 1 and stitch down at 2; continue to desired length of line. Bring ribbon back up at A, close to end of last stitch. Wrap by slipping needle once or twice under the stitch. Continue in this manner and stitch down to end.

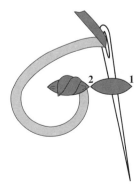

Using the Ribbon Embroidery Motifs

The ribbon embroidery motifs, #91 to 101, have been designed using 4mm and 7mm ribbons. The stitched examples on the back cover and the stitching guides on the following pages are shown actual size. Instructions for the stitches used in the motifs can be found on pages 59 to 63.

You may work any motif in a free-form manner, or you may draw a design outline directly on the background fabric. Place fabric directly over the design and trace with a water-soluble fabric marking pen. If the fabric is heavy, a lightbox will be helpful. You can also use a #2 lead pencil (for light to medium-colored fabrics) or a white pencil (for dark fabrics). You may also work ribbon embroidery with just position marks on the fabric, rather than a full pattern.

If desired, you can enlarge or reduce any of the motifs as long as you remember the limitations of the ribbon width. To enlarge, you can add more stitches or change to a wider ribbon, whichever looks best. To reduce, you can use a more narrow ribbon or take smaller (or fewer) stitches and/or pull the stitches more tightly. Always test-stitch a prototype of the new size on scrap fabric before incorporating it into your design.

If you wish to work in different colors to match the particular color scheme of your crazy quilt, feel free to do so.

91 Trail of Roses

Note: *Use assorted colors for the Spider Web Roses.*

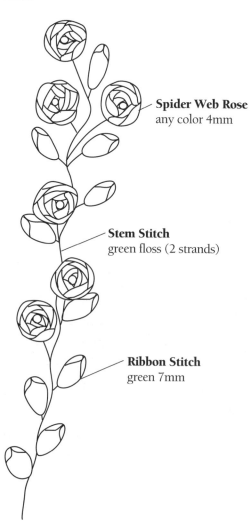

Spider Web Rose
any color 4mm

Stem Stitch
green floss (2 strands)

Ribbon Stitch
green 7mm

92 *Bouquet of Flowers*

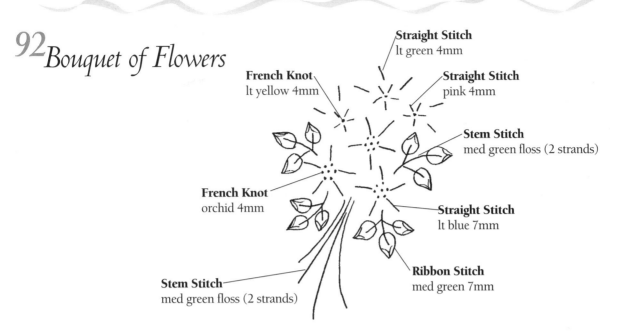

Straight Stitch
lt green 4mm

French Knot
lt yellow 4mm

Straight Stitch
pink 4mm

Stem Stitch
med green floss (2 strands)

French Knot
orchid 4mm

Straight Stitch
lt blue 7mm

Ribbon Stitch
med green 7mm

Stem Stitch
med green floss (2 strands)

93 *Flower Basket*

Note: *Do Weaving for basket first; add base and handle using Wrapped Backstitch. Fill with flowers and leaves. Make Loop Stitch bow on handle last.*

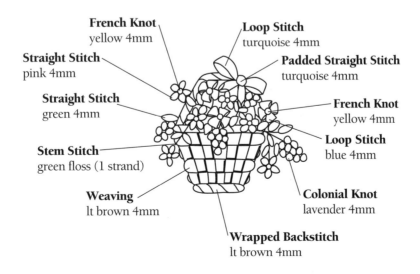

French Knot
yellow 4mm

Loop Stitch
turquoise 4mm

Straight Stitch
pink 4mm

Padded Straight Stitch
turquoise 4mm

Straight Stitch
green 4mm

French Knot
yellow 4mm

Stem Stitch
green floss (1 strand)

Loop Stitch
blue 4mm

Weaving
lt brown 4mm

Colonial Knot
lavender 4mm

Wrapped Backstitch
lt brown 4mm

94 Spiraling Roses

Note: *Work each Spider Web Rose with two colors: the center Spider Web Rose is dk fuchsia surrounded by med fuchsia; add gold French Knot in center; the four corner Spider Web Roses are med fuchsia surrounded by pink. Add yellow French Knot in center of each.*

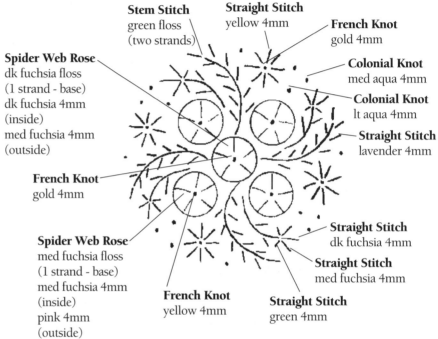

Stem Stitch
green floss
(two strands)

Straight Stitch
yellow 4mm

French Knot
gold 4mm

Colonial Knot
med aqua 4mm

Colonial Knot
lt aqua 4mm

Straight Stitch
lavender 4mm

Spider Web Rose
dk fuchsia floss
(1 strand - base)
dk fuchsia 4mm
(inside)
med fuchsia 4mm
(outside)

French Knot
gold 4mm

Straight Stitch
dk fuchsia 4mm

Straight Stitch
med fuchsia 4mm

Spider Web Rose
med fuchsia floss
(1 strand - base)
med fuchsia 4mm
(inside)
pink 4mm
(outside)

French Knot
yellow 4mm

Straight Stitch
green 4mm

95 Butterfly

Note: *Work Wrapped Backstitch body first, followed by top wings and bottom wings last. Add antennae.*

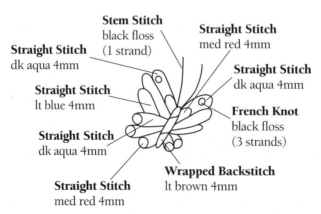

Stem Stitch
black floss
(1 strand)

Straight Stitch
med red 4mm

Straight Stitch
dk aqua 4mm

Straight Stitch
lt blue 4mm

Straight Stitch
dk aqua 4mm

French Knot
black floss
(3 strands)

Straight Stitch
dk aqua 4mm

Straight Stitch
med red 4mm

Wrapped Backstitch
lt brown 4mm

96 Rose Wreath

Note: *Work the Woven Ribbon pattern first, then anchor each intersection with a French Knot.*

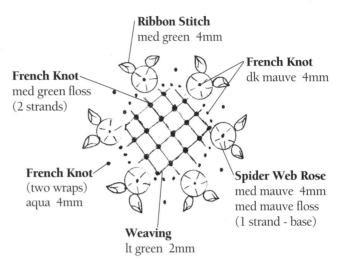

Ribbon Stitch
med green 4mm

French Knot
med green floss
(2 strands)

French Knot
dk mauve 4mm

French Knot
(two wraps)
aqua 4mm

Weaving
lt green 2mm

Spider Web Rose
med mauve 4mm
med mauve floss
(1 strand - base)

97 Bluebird

Note: *Work stitches in the following order: breast, tails, head, wing, eye, beak and foot.*

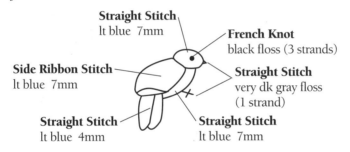

Straight Stitch
lt blue 7mm

French Knot
black floss (3 strands)

Side Ribbon Stitch
lt blue 7mm

Straight Stitch
very dk gray floss
(1 strand)

Straight Stitch
lt blue 4mm

Straight Stitch
lt blue 7mm

98 Heart Wreath

Note: *Work Stem Stitch heart shape first, then add flowers and leaves.*

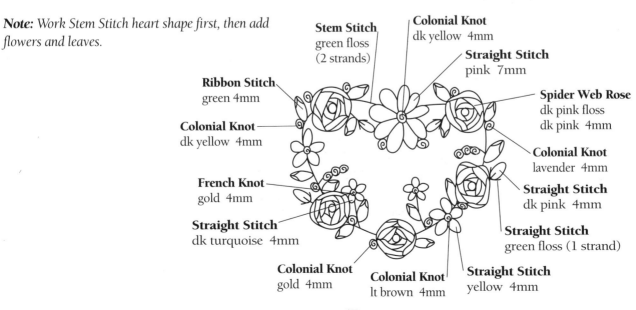

Stem Stitch
green floss
(2 strands)

Colonial Knot
dk yellow 4mm

Straight Stitch
pink 7mm

Ribbon Stitch
green 4mm

Spider Web Rose
dk pink floss
dk pink 4mm

Colonial Knot
dk yellow 4mm

Colonial Knot
lavender 4mm

French Knot
gold 4mm

Straight Stitch
dk pink 4mm

Straight Stitch
dk turquoise 4mm

Straight Stitch
green floss (1 strand)

Colonial Knot
gold 4mm

Colonial Knot
lt brown 4mm

Straight Stitch
yellow 4mm

99 Spider and Web

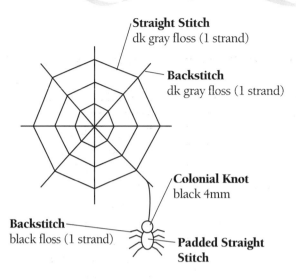

Straight Stitch
dk gray floss (1 strand)

Backstitch
dk gray floss (1 strand)

Colonial Knot
black 4mm

Backstitch
black floss (1 strand)

Padded Straight Stitch

100 Hummingbird

Note: *Work hummingbird in the following order:*
body, head, tail, back feathers (including cap on head),
wings, eye and beak.

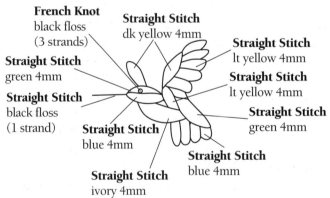

French Knot
black floss
(3 strands)

Straight Stitch
dk yellow 4mm

Straight Stitch
lt yellow 4mm

Straight Stitch
green 4mm

Straight Stitch
lt yellow 4mm

Straight Stitch
black floss
(1 strand)

Straight Stitch
green 4mm

Straight Stitch
blue 4mm

Straight Stitch
blue 4mm

Straight Stitch
ivory 4mm

101 Petite Rose

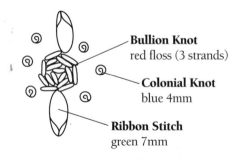

Bullion Knot
red floss (3 strands)

Colonial Knot
blue 4mm

Ribbon Stitch
green 7mm